HOW TO
GET THROUGH
WHAT YOU'LL NEVER
GET O

Walki
by tr

BILL PRATER

First published in 2022 by Striving Together Publications, a ministry of Lancaster Baptist Church, Lancaster, CA 93535. Striving Together Publications is committed to providing tried, trusted, and proven resources that will further equip local churches to carry out the Great Commission. Your comments and suggestions are valued.

Striving Together Publications
4020 E. Lancaster Blvd.
Lancaster, CA 93535
800.201.7748
strivingtogether.com

The author and publication team have put forth every effort to give proper credit to quotes and thoughts that are not original with the author. It is not our intent to claim originality with any quote or thought that could not readily be tied to an original source.

ISBN 978-1-59894-487-7 (paperback)
ISBN 978-1-59894-488-4 (ebook)
Printed in the United States of America

CONTENTS

T. J.

GRIEF. FOR THOSE WHO have experienced it, even the word hurts.

The pain of grief comes in many forms. Sometimes it's a gut punch. Sometimes it lingers as a deep soul ache. Sometimes it runs like a searing pain directly through your chest. Often, it comes to stay.

But as long as we live in this fallen world, we'll experience the losses that invite grief.

- Loss of health
- Loss of a job
- Loss of the future we had so carefully planned
- Loss of a relationship

- Loss of a marriage
- Loss of a dream
- Loss of a family member

All of these losses sound bad when you hear about them in the lives of others. But when that loss enters your own life, it leaves you grief-stricken.

Such was the case for our family on February 6, 2018. I was sitting up in our bed that evening when my phone rang. I saw on the screen that the call was from our daughter-in-law, Sheena, the wife of our oldest son, T. J. In the brief second between seeing Sheena's name and answering the phone, I considered that since Sheena rarely called me but usually my wife Katie, it would probably be T. J. on the other end. Perhaps he had misplaced his phone and was using Sheena's to reach me.

But it wasn't T. J. It was Sheena, and she was crying. She asked me to put her on speaker phone so she could talk to both Katie and me together. We gathered together to hear the worst news we could imagine: T. J. was dead. He had just been killed in a freak accident while working underneath his pickup in the driveway of their home.

The news crushed us. I couldn't breath or speak. T. J. was gone? It didn't seem possible. Not even believable.

Katie and I were proud of T. J. He was everything a parent could hope for. He loved God fervently. He loved his wife tenderly and was a fantastic father to their three daughters, Malorie Paige, Ellie Grace, and Callie Mae. T. J. owned his own business, and it was flourishing. But his real passion was for the Lord, his family, and his church. He sacrificially served his church family as a layman. T. J. was exactly what people mean when they describe someone as a "good guy." To know T. J. was to love T. J.

The shock and pain of that initial news was staggering. I couldn't believe it was real. It felt like a bad dream, but when I woke up it was still there. And the next day it was still there. And the next. And the day after that.

Over the years, as a pastor to our church family and a chaplain for our law enforcement community, I have had many occasions to comfort grieving families. But this was the first time that I had experienced such a loss myself. My son was gone.

I think the first thing that surprised me about grief was its intensity. It's not just something you hold at arm's length and examine, the way you would a part for your car or knick-knack for your desk. It's gripping, consuming. Sharp and deadening all at the same time.

The next thing that surprised me about grief was its longevity. It doesn't go away in a week. It doesn't go away in "the coming days" after the funeral as well-meaning people pray during a memorial service. In some ways, it still hasn't gone away.

Yes, the initial shock and unrelenting pain has subsided with time. But there are still moments when it washes over me again fresh and real. Sometimes these moments come out of nowhere. I see a father and his son in the hardware store and suddenly miss T. J. as if I had just lost him that morning. A family picture. An expression one of our granddaughter makes that reminds me of her dad. But sometimes these moments are more expected: Mother's Day and Father's Day, Thanksgiving and Christmas, his December 3 birthday, and, of course, February 6.

The loss of T. J. is one Katie and I will never get over. And honestly, I don't want to. T. J. was too important to me to pretend as if life just goes on the same with or without him.

But although we won't just get over the loss of our son, God has so graciously comforted and helped us learn to get *through* it.

Ours is not the only loss in this world. If you're reading these pages, most likely you, too, are dealing with loss and grief…or someone you love is. I will be honest with you: I don't have all the answers. I still have many questions, and I'm still learning. But I do have some truths from God's Word that have become precious to me through the gut-wrenching journey of our experience. I pray that, for whatever grief and loss you may be experiencing, this short book brings a balm to your soul and courage to your heart.

CHAPTER ONE

You Don't Have to Get Over It

Shortly after T. J.'s death, a pastor friend from another state reached out to me. He, too, had experienced a tragic loss in the death of his grandson several years prior, and the words he shared with me that day helped me: "You don't have to get over it."

That simple statement lifted a load. It seems we have an expectation—for ourselves or others—that after a certain amount of time we should be able to close the door on grief, turn from our loss, and move on as if it didn't happen. This is not only unrealistic, but it's also foolish and prevents us from experiencing the ongoing grace of God in our ongoing loss.

This statement by my friend brought me to a passage that has become precious to me. It's a personal and transparent testimony from the apostle Paul of a difficulty in his life that he never "got over."

> And lest I should be exalted above measure through the abundance of the revelations, there was given to me a thorn in the flesh, the messenger of Satan to buffet me, lest I should be exalted above measure. For this thing I besought the Lord thrice, that it might depart from me. And he said unto me, My grace is sufficient for thee: for my strength is made perfect in weakness. Most gladly therefore will I rather glory in my infirmities, that the power of Christ may rest upon me. Therefore I take pleasure in infirmities, in reproaches, in necessities, in persecutions, in distresses for Christ's sake: for when I am weak, then am I strong. (2 Corinthians 12:7–10)

Paul never revealed the exact nature of his "thorn in the flesh," but it was a problem that was serious enough to cause him great suffering. Some people think it may have been trouble with his eyes, which for a scholar and writer like Paul would have been a great handicap. I think that perhaps Paul was vague in his wording because he wanted us to focus more on the principle of receiving God's grace for whatever we need it for than on the specifics of his own trial. But whatever this thorn was, it was something that Paul didn't want but had to live with. Whatever the case, it drove Paul to his knees to beseech the Lord for relief.

Assuming Paul was afflicted with his thorn in the flesh immediately or soon after receiving the visions and revelations he mentioned at the beginning of chapter 12, means that at the time he wrote this letter to the Corinthian church, he had already dealt with the thorn for fourteen years. And I think it's safe to say that he continued to deal with it for the rest of his life. He never got over it. Furthermore, God didn't ask him to.

There are many well-meaning people who encourage those who have suffered a great loss to get over it. Perhaps some of them have talked to you. Or perhaps you have had your own thoughts, "Shouldn't I have gotten over this by now?" Perhaps you feel guilt that you still feel grief.

In actuality, however, the entire concept of assuming people should just get over every type of loss is a misleading and empty expectation.

Think about it in terms of physical challenges. Recently, I was mowing my grass, happened to step wrong, and twisted my ankle. I immediately fell to the ground writhing in pain, but eventually I was able to stand up and walk it off. But let's say that it had gotten worse instead of better, so I ended up in the hospital with an infection in my foot that was rapidly spreading up my leg, and in order to save my life they had to amputate my leg. That's not something I could just shake off. And it doesn't matter how long I lived after that, I would never get over it because I would be reminded of it every morning when I woke up and saw the nub. Rather than getting over it, I would have to learn to adjust to a new reality.

A loss, like the one our family suffered, and perhaps like you have suffered, is more like an amputation than a sprain. And you don't get over an amputation.

Here's another angle that shows the faulty expectation of just getting over loss: We don't look at people who are experiencing life's joys and tell them to just get over it. So why do we assume people should just get over life's sorrows?

For example, let's say some friends of yours are blessed with a child, and you send them a nice card that says, "Congratulations on the birth of your new baby." Then five years later you get an invitation in the mail to that child's birthday party. Who opens that invitation and says, "Another birthday party? Seriously? This is like five years in a row. Hey, we get it. You have a kid and you've had him for five years, but honestly, you really need to just get over it."

We don't expect people to get over the birth of a child, so why should we expect them to get over the death of one? We don't expect people to get over the joys of life, so why should we expect them get over the sorrows?

Jerry Sittser lost his wife, his daughter, and his mother all in the same car wreck. In his book, *A Grace Disguised*, he writes,

> Can anyone really expect to recover from such tragedy, considering the value of what was lost and the consequences of that loss? Recovery is a misleading and empty expectation. We recover from broken limbs, not amputations. Catastrophic loss by definition precludes recovery. It will transform us or destroy us, but it will never leave us the same. There is no going back to the past, which is gone forever, only going ahead to the future, which has yet to be discovered. Whatever that future is, it will, and must, include the pain of the past with it. Sorrow never entirely leaves the soul of those who have suffered a severe loss. If anything, it may keep going deeper.[1]

Dean Herring, my pastor friend who first told me that I didn't have to "get over" T. J.'s death wrote along these lines on an anniversary of his grandson's death:

The notion that suddenly (or eventually) the sorrow somehow dissipates is a fable that has been created by the empty slogans of people who have never suffered deep loss. Why do we feel ashamed of sorrow as though it is some sort of leprous emotion? Why do we hide our tears when our Savior wept openly at the death of a friend? The ability to sorrow and weep is a gift from God and is a sure sign of a living heart and a greater love. The pain remains and the tears come like rogue waves, but God has somehow enabled us all to live through the unthinkable. We are here. We live on in our sorrow and with our pain. We live in His grace.[2]

When you're dealing with the loss of someone or something you love, God isn't calling you to just get over it. He's inviting you to receive His sufficient grace.

There is a difference between getting *over* a loss and getting *through* it. You may never get over the loss you are currently going through—I will never get over the loss of my son—but, by God's grace, you can get through it.

What does getting through a loss look like? I think the best word to describe it is *acceptance.* Acceptance doesn't mean that everything is okay. It simply means that *you* are okay and that you are discovering God's grace as a supply in your sorrow.

Getting *over* a loss is moving on as if the loss had never happened—shutting the door behind you and doing your best to pretend the pain away. Getting *through* a loss, however, is reaching a place where you accept the horrible events that brought so much grief and sorrow, while finding the strength through God's grace to continue forward in life despite the loss.

For Paul, reaching that place of acceptance seems to have come after three protracted seasons of prayer that God would remove his thorn. "For this thing I besought the Lord thrice, that it might depart from me" (2 Corinthians 12:8). In my observation, reaching this point of acceptance comes at different times for different people. The important thing is not to count the days until we can flip a switch and start moving through. The important thing is God's grace and learning to lean on it day by day. In time, God's grace will enable us to accept the reality of our loss as well as the reality of God's daily strength.

Even as God denied Paul's requests to remove this thorn in the flesh, He didn't expect Paul to just deal with the thorn himself. He didn't expect Paul to just get over it, toughen up, and pretend it was no longer an issue. Rather, He invited Paul to lean on Him for abundant, sufficient grace.

And although Paul never got over his thorn in the flesh, he did continue serving the Lord through it, and by God's grace, he found strength to move forward in his life in spite of it. I believe we see that in Paul's response to God's promise of sufficient grace: "Most gladly therefore will I rather glory in my infirmities, that the power of Christ may rest upon me" (2 Corinthians 12:9) Paul found the strength to move forward, not by his own will or power, but by the grace of God.

CHAPTER TWO

The God Who Gives Grace and Strength

TRAGEDY WILL CHALLENGE EVERYTHING you have ever believed about God. Even truths that you assumed you stood firmly on—simple truths like God is good, God is faithful, God cares for me—feel questionable. But if we are to receive the grace God offers in grief, we must believe rightly about the God who gives this grace. Otherwise, we won't want it or trust Him to receive it.

One of the clear truths the Bible reveals about God is that He is sovereign—He is the ultimate ruler of everything. In human terms, a "sovereign" is a king or queen. To say God is sovereign means He has the power, wisdom, and authority to do or allow anything He chooses with regard to His creation.

The LORD hath prepared his throne in the heavens; and his kingdom ruleth over all. (Psalm 103:19)

But our God is in the heavens: he hath done whatsoever he hath pleased. (Psalm 115:3)

Whatsoever the LORD pleased, that did he in heaven, and in earth, in the seas, and all deep places. (Psalm 135:6)

Thine, O LORD, is the greatness, and the power, and the glory, and the victory, and the majesty: for all that is in the heaven and in the earth is thine; thine is the kingdom, O LORD, and thou art exalted as head above all. Both riches and honour come of thee, and thou reignest over all; and in thine hand is power and might; and in thine hand it is to make great, and to give strength unto all. (1 Chronicles 29:11–12)

> Remember the former things of old: for I am God,
> and there is none else; I am God, and there is none
> like me, Declaring the end from the beginning, and
> from ancient times the things that are not yet done,
> saying, My counsel shall stand, and I will do all my
> pleasure: (Isaiah 46:9–10)

The good thing about God's sovereignty is that *God* is good. So His purposes in all that He does are good.

I believe we see Paul's acceptance of God's sovereignty in the words he used to describe the way he received his thorn in the flesh. Notice the word *given*:

> And lest I should be exalted above measure through
> the abundance of the revelations, there was given
> to me a thorn in the flesh, the messenger of Satan
> to buffet me, lest I should be exalted above measure.
> (2 Corinthians 12:7)

Paul knew that, at some level, this thorn came as Satan's attack—"the messenger of Satan to buffet me." But he also recognized that in a larger sense, what came into his life could only be what God allowed. Thus it was "given" him through God's permission.

Counterintuitive as it may seem, there is comfort in realizing that the grief that God allows into our lives is not just a stroke of bad luck or happenchance. It is part of God's divine design to work in our lives to bring about good.

Adoniram Judson, the first American missionary to the country of Burma (modern-day Myanmar) faced wave after wave of unrelenting sorrow. He and his young wife lost three children, then during the Anglo-Burmese war, he was imprisoned in torturous and inhuman conditions for eighteen months. Shortly after his release, his wife Ann died. Judson wrote to his sister back in the States, "If I had not felt certain that every additional trial was ordered by infinite love and mercy, I could not have survived my accumulated sufferings."[3] It was Judson's belief in the sovereignty of God that spared him the unbearable thought that he was simply an unlucky man who had given his life to the spread of the gospel, only to be abandoned by God to the whims of chance. Knowing that God—a loving, merciful God—was in control and allowed only the suffering that was for Judson's ultimate good gave purpose to Judson's pain. It can to yours as well.

Sometimes we give lip service to God's sovereignty, but then when He exercises it, we accuse Him of being unfair or unloving. We want God to be in control—but only as long as His purposes align with ours. That's not really trust in God; it's trust in ourselves. A true belief in God's sovereignty is to believe that God is never caught by surprise. He is always in control even through events that seem random and meaningless. He is King, and as such is not required to explain His actions to us. And a true belief in God's goodness holds to the conviction that even when God exercises His sovereignty in ways that don't seem right to us, He is good and has our best interests at heart.

So if we're going to receive grace from our good and sovereign God, we need a firm understanding of basic Bible truths about God and His perspective.

God Sees What We Don't See

In 1968, the crew of Apollo 8 flew to the moon and circled it ten times. As they looked down from almost 250,000 miles away, they had a different perspective on Earth than anyone present on the planet did. Things that seemed large to people on the ground were invisible from space. At the same time, things that were too large to see from the ground could be clearly seen by the astronauts as they looked down. They had a unique perspective that only a handful of people have ever seen. That perspective brought such a sense of awe in God's power that the crew read the creation account from Genesis 1 on a broadcast from their spaceship.

When we look at our problems, they seem huge. I suppose there are times when we exaggerate or magnify our problems beyond their actual size. But there are also times—the kind of times that bring devastating grief—that our problems really are severe. Yet, from God's eternal perspective, He can see the larger picture. If we only view our suffering and pain from the limited perspective of the moment, we will conclude that it is just not fair. If we continue in that thinking, we will be tempted to become bitter and resentful toward God. If we allow that resentment to grow, our hearts will be hardened, and we will become stuck in our grief. We must learn to trust that God sees and knows what is best, even if it is not what we would choose for ourselves.

Earlier in the same letter in which Paul told about his thorn in the flesh, he described an important perspective on suffering:

> For which cause we faint not; but though our outward man perish, yet the inward man is renewed day by day. For our light affliction, which is but for a moment, worketh for us a far more exceeding and eternal weight of glory; While we look not at the things which are seen, but at the things which are not seen: for the things which are seen are temporal; but the things which are not seen are eternal. (2 Corinthians 4:16–18)

Paul endured suffering that would make most of us quit because he was not looking at it from an earthly perspective, but rather an eternal perspective. This requires faith in God's promises and in God Himself.

It sounds simple to say, but it's important to come back to God during days of blinding grief: we know who God is through His Word. There are times when our perception of God and our feelings about Him are skewed or flawed. At these times, we must remind ourselves of who the Bible declares God to be. For instance, God is

- Good (Psalm 100:5)
- Longsuffering (2 Peter 3:9)
- Merciful (Psalm 130:7)
- Loving (1 John 4:8)
- Patient (Nehemiah 9:17)
- Kind (Psalm 63:3)
- Ever present (Psalm 139:7–12)
- A refuge in times of trouble (Psalm 46:1)

None of these realties about God changed the night T. J. died. God was just as good and loving after that night as He was before. None of His characteristics changed in the days, weeks, months and years that followed as we tried to deal with our grief and loss. And none of that will *ever* change. Our suffering is not proof that God has failed or changed or lost interest in us. God will always and forever be who He eternally has been. He sees what we cannot see from our limited perspective, and He knows what is best for us.

God Allows What We Wouldn't Allow

If we were in charge we would do things differently. But we are not in charge. God's plans are not only different from our plans; they are also better. God's plans can be trusted because God is good, and He knows more than we do. We often will not understand at the time what is going on. Vance Havner, a twentieth-century revival preacher, used to say, "God marks across some of our days, 'Will explain later.'"[4]

There are some things we will never understand in this life. Job repeatedly questioned why he was suffering so greatly. His friends accused him of having hidden sin in his life. Job said that if he got an audience with God he would demand answers. Yet when God did speak with Job, it was God who had the questions, and Job had nothing to say except to confess his shortcoming. "Wherefore I abhor myself, and repent in dust and ashes" (Job 42:6). God never explained to Job why He allowed Satan to strike his life so cruelly, yet through Job's life, we see God's merciful care and ability to sustain us through suffering. James 5:11 says, "Behold, we count them happy which endure. Ye have heard of the patience of Job, and have seen the end of the Lord; that the Lord is very pitiful, and of tender mercy." We don't have to have all the answers to trust God.

It seems that Paul's thorn in the flesh never went away, but the more that he relied on God rather than himself, the more strength he had to handle the pain in his life. The pain didn't decrease, but God's grace increased to meet it. Paul was able to bear the weight because he had learned, "when I am weak, then am I strong." The longer he lived and the more he experienced God's grace in all types of suffering, the more beautiful God's plan became.

That has been true for others as well. The longer they have lived beyond their heartache and heartbreak, the clearer and more beautiful the picture of God's plan has become.

God Has What We Don't Have

Not only does God see what we don't see and allow what we wouldn't allow, but he has what we don't have—grace and strength. What's better, He gives these to us freely and abundantly.

God told Paul that His grace was *sufficient*. That means grace would supply everything that Paul needed—not so the pain would go away, but so he could accept it and still move forward.

I know how much we hurt when T. J. died. If it were not for God's grace and strength, I have no idea how we would have ever moved forward in our journey. The pain of losing our son was greater than anything I can even begin to describe, but the help we have received from the Lord is greater than I could begin to explain.

Our suffering is not unique. Many others have experienced great grief and loss and have also found God's grace sufficient. Born just after the Civil War, Annie Johnson Flint lost both of her parents when she was a young child. She developed a crippling arthritis while still a teenager. Much of her life she was bedridden. She knew pain and hardship and suffering all of her days. Yet in her pain, she discovered the reality of God's sufficient grace and penned these words:

> He giveth more grace as the burdens grow greater,
> He sendeth more strength as the labors increase,
> To added afflictions He addeth His mercy,
> To multiplied trials His multiplied peace.
>
> His Love has no limit; His grace has no measure,
> His pow'r has no boundary known unto men,
> For out of His infinite riches in Jesus,
> He giveth, and giveth, and giveth again!

Grace is God's supply for our every need, at the moment we need it. God does not give us everything we want. Every parent knows that doing that with a child is a recipe for disaster. They have not yet developed their judgment enough to know what is best for them. But parents who love their children provide everything possible to meet their children's needs, even if it requires great sacrifice to the parent. During the horrible first winter the Pilgrims spent at Plymouth, death from cold and hunger decimated the community. The group with the highest death rate was mothers who had small children. They gave up their very lives, forgoing food and warmth so that their children would survive.

Some people say that God never brings a trial into our lives that we cannot bear. That isn't really true. God brings lots of trials into our lives that are greater than our human strength and endurance can handle. It's more accurate to say that God never brings a trial into our lives that His grace cannot strengthen us to bear. He does not abandon us in our need. He does not run out of grace if a bunch of people ask for help all at once. He does not run out of patience if we come back to Him again and again seeking His help.

One author compared God's inexhaustible supply of grace to the never-ending waves falling on the beach.

No sooner will one wave crash into the sand than another appears. Then another, then another. This is a picture of God's sufficient grace. *Grace* is simply another word for God's tumbling, rumbling reservoir of strength and protection. It comes at us not occasionally or miserly but constantly and aggressively, wave upon wave. We've barely regained our balance from one breaker, and then, *bam,* here comes another....

We dare to hang our hat and stake our hope on the gladdest news of all: if God permits the challenge, he will provide the grace to meet it.

We never exhaust his supply. "Stop asking so much! My grace reservoir is running dry." Heaven knows no such words. God has enough grace to solve every dilemma you face, wipe every tear you cry, and answer every question you ask.

Would we expect anything less from God?[5]

I have searched diligently for an adequate description of God's grace, but the best way I can describe it is that it is "His supply for our every need when we need it." Grace is enough—always and forever enough. Christ provides the grace we need for every day of our lives. "And of his fulness have all we received, and grace for grace" (John 1:16).

John Newton penned what is probably the best-known hymn in the world: "Amazing Grace." His own life is a powerful testimony to the truth of the words. A man who had been a profane and immoral slave trader became a powerful preacher, and one of the key voices in the fight for the abolition of slavery. Newton did not just know God's grace theoretically; he knew it personally. First, he knew it in his salvation, but over the years, he also experienced it in his suffering. Perhaps the greatest trial of John's life was when his beloved wife Mary died. Even then, he reached for God's grace and found it sufficient. It was enough to sustain him and to enable him to continue his pastoral ministry.

Newton wrote, "The Bank of England is too poor to compensate for such a loss as mine. But the Lord, the all-sufficient God speaks, and it is done. Let those who know Him, and trust Him, be of good courage. He can give them strength according to their day. He can increase their strength as their trials increase... and what He can do He has promised that He will do."

In one stanza of "Amazing Grace," Newton testified,

Through many dangers, toils and snares
I have already come;
'Tis grace that brought me safe thus far,
And grace will lead me home.

God Can Use Pain for Our Good and His Glory

Romans 8:28 is one of the most precious promises in the Bible: "And we know that all things work together for good to them that love God, to them who are the called according to his purpose." Many of us have shared that verse with others who were going through a time of pain and loss. When it's your "all things" it's hard to understand how this promise can be true. After wrestling with this for some time, I came to the conclusion that God has a different definition of "good" than I do. My definition is immediate gratification; His definition is my eternal good and His eternal glory.

- My "good" would never include losing our son, and especially not in the prime of his life.
- My "good" would never include our daughter-in-law Sheena having to answer questions like, "Mommy, when is Jesus going to fix Daddy and bring him home?"
- My "good" would be T. J. alive and calling me every week, without fail, just to see how I was doing.
- My "good" would be a kiss on my bald head and the words, "Love ya, Pops."
- My "good" would be T. J. getting to watch all three of his daughters grow up to be godly ladies who marry godly men and spend their lives serving the God their mom and dad served.

Knowing that God has a different definition for good than we have is helpful because it encourages us to look for purpose in our times of tragedy, pain, and loss.

Mary Winslow came to the United States in 1815, knowing that her husband, Thomas, would soon join her and their children. But before Thomas set sail, he died suddenly, leaving Mary a widow with nine children to raise alone in a new country. Her faith and trust in God saw the needs of the family met, and she went on to write a number of books that inspired many. In one she coined the phrase, "Adversity the school of love." She went on to describe, "If we wish to know much of the reality and worth of God's love, we must experience and feel real adversity."[6]

What do we find when we are enrolled in the school of adversity? In what ways does God use pain for our good and His glory? We will never understand all of God's purposes this side of Heaven, but here are a few.

Pain produces a deeper relationship with the Lord.

> "And not only so, but we glory in tribulations also: knowing that tribulation worketh patience; And patience, experience; and experience, hope: And hope maketh not ashamed; because the love of God is shed abroad in our hearts by the Holy Ghost which is given unto us." (Romans 5:3–5)

Granted, when we suffer pain, we often wonder why God couldn't teach us these lessons in a kinder, more gentle way. We ask, "Did we really need to suffer like this to grow?" The answer is yes. God loves us too much to put us through pain without purpose. I will be the first to admit, I don't understand why God does what He does, but I do know He loves me and wants me to draw near to Him, and sometimes He will allow me to feel the pain of this world's unhealed hurts if it brings us closer. One author said, "Our deepest encounters with God may come wrapped in the deepest pains of life."[7]

Even when our pain is a consequence for a sinful choice on our part (as it sometimes, but not always, is), God still desires to use it to deepen our relationship with Him. The Bible tells us about the chastening God brings into the lives of His children when our hearts stray from Him: "Now no chastening for the present seemeth to be joyous, but grievous: nevertheless afterward it yieldeth the peaceable fruit of righteousness unto them which are exercised thereby" (Hebrews 12:11). We should never assume that someone else's suffering is the chastening hand of God. And even in our suffering, we should be quick to repent if and when the Lord brings personal sin to our attention. This doesn't mean that the entire loss of the situation was brought on by our sin. It simply means that one of the ways God uses grief is to expose to us the sinful tendencies that were already present in our own hearts. As we become aware of these and turn to the Lord in humble repentance, we find a sweetness in dependance upon Him that we did not previously know.

One of the ways that pain produces a deeper relationship with the Lord is in the purification of our faith. Writing to suffering Christians, the apostle Peter encouraged them, "Wherein ye greatly rejoice, though now for a season, if need be, ye are in heaviness through manifold temptations: That the trial of your faith, being much more precious than of gold that perisheth, though it be tried with fire, might be found unto praise and honour and glory at the appearing of Jesus Christ" (1 Peter 1:6–7). Before suffering, our untested faith may say "God is always good" as a glib phrase. But as grief envelops us and we lean into the truths of who God is because of what the Bible says—even when we don't see it—our convictions of God's goodness and faithfulness are stripped of sentimentality, and our faith is purified and strengthened.

Speaking of the way suffering brings us closer to the Lord, Charles Spurgeon reportedly said, "I have learned to kiss the waves that throw me up against the Rock of Ages."

Pain conforms us into the image of Christ.

My brethren, count it all joy when ye fall into divers temptations; Knowing this, that the trying of your faith worketh patience. But let patience have her perfect work, that ye may be perfect and entire, wanting nothing. (James 1:2–4)

The testing of our faith can bring a spiritual maturity that nothing else can bring.

For more than twenty-five years, a massive block of marble sat outside Florence, Italy. Two different sculptors had tried and failed to turn it into a statue of David. When Michelangelo was tasked with completing the project, he took a flawed block of mediocre marble and turned it into what has become the most famous statue in the world. Again and again, the noted sculptor struck the rock, striking off piece after piece until the figure of David was complete.

Think back to Romans 8:28: "And we know that all things work together for good to them that love God, to them who are the called according to his purpose." Sometimes we act as if this passage ends right here.

But the very next verse describes the good God brings into our lives and the purpose He is committed to working out: "For whom he did foreknow, he also did predestinate to be conformed to the image of his Son, that he might be the firstborn among many brethren." God's purpose in your life is to make you like Jesus. God is going to chisel away all that distracts from Christ in you so that His glory may be seen through you.

This process of becoming like Christ is not painless or easy. But neither was it easy for the Lord to lay aside the glory of Heaven and take on the limitations of a human body. It was not easy for Him to suffer the abuse, humiliation and pain of the cross. It was not easy for Him to take our sins and pay the price He did not owe. Why would we think it would be easy and painless to become more like Him?

The process is painful, but the result is beautiful. We can trust God as the perfect sculptor of our lives.

Pain in our life equips us to help others with pain in their lives.

> "Blessed be God, even the Father of our Lord Jesus Christ, the Father of mercies, and the God of all comfort; Who comforteth us in all our tribulation, that we may be able to comfort them which are in any trouble, by the comfort wherewith we ourselves are comforted of God. (2 Corinthians 1:3–4)

There are days, especially in the first stages of grief when it feels like the sun is never going to shine again. There is this darkness and sense of despair. One of the things that can relieve the rawness of pain and the overwhelming confusion is for someone else who has suffered a loss but is further along the path of acceptance to come and share their experiences of God's comfort with us.

The story goes that when Victoria was Queen of England, she heard of a young mother who had lost a child. Victoria had lost her beloved husband not long before, so she went to visit the bereaved family. After she left, the neighbors wanted to know what she said. "Nothing," the mother replied. "She put her hands on mine, and we wept together."

As much as God has allowed, Katie and I have tried to use our experience to help others, just as others thankfully used their experience to help us. Likewise, when we share from our experience with those whose lives have been recently shattered, it not only encourages them, but it helps us gain perspective by realizing how far we've come.

Receiving God's Grace and Strength

Because of the reality of God's sovereignty and the grace and strength that He so freely gives us, we can confidently say, "Even when our *circumstances* aren't good, God's *purposes* are good."

But even when we know these truths in our heads, sometimes we struggle to hold them in our daily responses. How do we receive God's grace and strength? The short answer is faith. We simply take

God at His word and reach for the strength He has promised moment by moment as we need it.

But the longer answer includes a few tools God has given us through His Word. I would like to share those with you in our next chapter.

CHAPTER THREE

Responding to God's Grace

Have you ever seen someone who is drowning and in need of rescue? They often flail their bodies wildly and sometimes, in their confused panic, even fight their rescuers.

Grief can give you the sensation of drowning. No wonder, then, that so many people respond in ways that ultimately push away the grace God desires to give them. They are confused and flailing for hope, not realizing that without God's grace, their efforts are futile.

When Paul understood that God was not going to remove his thorn in the flesh, he made a simple choice that defined the rest of his life: "Most gladly therefore will I rather glory in my infirmities, that the power of Christ may rest upon me. Therefore I take pleasure in infirmities, in reproaches, in necessities, in persecutions, in distresses for Christ's sake: for when I am weak, then am I strong" (2 Corinthians 12:9–10). Paul did not simply rejoice in the reality of God's grace and strength in abstract theory. He chose to receive it and even rejoice in the needs that led him to it.

This brings us back to the necessity of acceptance. Remember, acceptance doesn't mean that everything is okay. It simply means that *you* are okay because you are depending on God's grace through your sorrow.

Resisting God's Grace

Consider the alternatives to acceptance. What do people do who don't receive the grace of God?

Some live in denial. While most of these people would never say the painful event didn't actually happen, they try to live as if it didn't happen. They simply put off what they really need to face. Perhaps they deny it by staying busy, so they don't have the time or the space to let the pain in. Others try to live as if nothing had changed. Denial does nothing to change the reality of the terrible tragedy they have suffered.

In *Great Expectations*, Charles Dickens describes this attempt to deal with grief in the sad life of the rich heiress Miss Havisham. Jilted on her wedding day, she insisted on wearing her wedding dress every day for the rest of her life. The remains of the wedding meal were left to rot on the table. She refused to acknowledge the passage of time, stopping all the clocks in the house at 8:40, the time she received the news that her intended groom was not coming.

Another form of denial is when people run from their pain through change. They may change jobs, spouses, or cities. Obviously, there are times that call for a move or job change, but to pursue change in an effort to hide from the past is both futile and damaging. Wherever we go, we take our pain with us, and no change of circumstances, people, or surroundings can take it away.

A loss is something terrible that cannot be changed. Denial does not change the past, nor does it provide real relief from the pain. You cannot deal with pain by not dealing with it. You cannot deal with the pain until you face it—not in your own strength, but in the power of God's grace.

Some try to drown the pain through indulgence. Some people try to find something to cover up the pain. Some turn to drugs or alcohol or immorality. Indeed, these things can briefly mask the pain. Proverbs 31:6–7 says, "Give strong drink unto him that is ready to perish, and wine unto those that be of heavy hearts. Let him drink, and forget his poverty, and remember his misery no more." But substance abuse is not a long-term solution and actually creates new problems. Proverbs warns of these dangers repeatedly.

> Wine is a mocker, strong drink is raging: and whosoever is deceived thereby is not wise. (Proverbs 20:1)

Who hath woe? who hath sorrow? who hath contentions? who hath babbling? who hath wounds without cause? who hath redness of eyes? They that tarry long at the wine; they that go to seek mixed wine. Look not thou upon the wine when it is red, when it giveth his colour in the cup, when it moveth itself aright. At the last it biteth like a serpent, and stingeth like an adder. (Proverbs 23:29–32)

As one person remarked, "You can't drown your sorrows because sorrows can swim." Indulging in pain-deadening vices compounds the suffering. Because the relief experienced is only temporary at best, people find themselves needing more and more of their indulgence of choice to find relief. Addiction often follows.

Some resort to anger. No one is happy about suffering pain and loss, and there may be a temptation to blame the person who caused the loss—or at least a person they can blame for the loss. The physical and emotional changes brought when we unleash anger can provide a temporary relief from the pain, but getting mad at someone does not change the loss, nor does it heal the hurting heart.

Sometimes an innocent person becomes the target of this grief-driven anger. Even though they had nothing to do with the loss, they become the victim of the hurting person's anger. Making other people feel worse will never make you feel better. Anger is natural, but it can also be exceedingly destructive—to you and to those around you.

Sometimes a grieving person's anger is directed toward God. Their reasoning is that because He is sovereign and all powerful, He could have stopped the loss from happening. I think all of us, even those of us who are convinced of the goodness and sovereignty of God, wrestle through these questions. And we aren't alone. When Jesus came to the home of his dear friends Mary, Martha, and Lazarus just after Lazarus had died, both Martha and Mary expressed their disappointment that Jesus had not kept Lazarus from dying. "Then said Martha unto Jesus, Lord, if thou hadst been here, my brother had not died. ... Then when Mary was come where Jesus was, and saw him, she fell down at his feet, saying unto him, Lord, if thou hadst been here, my brother had not died" (John 11:21, 32). Although their words were almost identical, it seems their tone was different. While Martha said these words as an accusation to the Lord, Mary said them through tears of worship.

God doesn't have to answer our questions about why He didn't overrule in the situations that have brought us such grief. It is likely that, because He can see what we cannot see, we wouldn't understand His purposes anyway. But we should beware of lashing out toward God in anger.

Some become bitter. Unchecked anger toward God leads to bitterness. Many people, when walking through suffering, become so filled with anger at God that they live in a prison of bitterness for the rest of their lives. Often, their spiritual life is never the same. And sadly, some follow the path carved out by their pain to a complete rejection of Christianity and unbelief. Bitterness never changes anything for the better.

One of the ways to fight bitterness is to focus on what's left, not what's lost. Of course, I'm in no way suggesting that someone should just forget what's happened (denial). That's not even possible. But sometimes we can let our painful memories so dominate our minds and viewpoints that our good memories all but disappear as they get tucked away in some dark corner of our minds. We combat this by spending our time reliving the good memories and refusing to let the painful ones drag us down.

One thing Katie and I have tried to be intentional about is remembering we have two other children and eight grandchildren who need us. The last thing we want to happen is for T. J.'s brother and sister to resent their brother's death because it has robbed them of *us*. Hebrews 12:15 warns us that bitterness doesn't just hurt us; it also hurts those around us: "Looking diligently lest any man fail of the grace of God; lest any root of bitterness springing up trouble you, *and thereby many be defiled.*"

Responding to God's Grace

None of our natural responses are healthy or productive, and they tend to build walls in our hearts that separate us from God and His grace. How can we instead respond to and receive God's grace?

Express your grief to the Lord. A crisis always produces strong emotions, and these feelings can be scary. So many times, we don't know what to do with them, but I think the most biblical way to deal with our emotions is to take them to the Lord in prayer. That's what so many authors of the psalms did. On numerous occasions they expressed their feelings of hopelessness, helplessness, sorrow, and loneliness. They even expressed feelings of abandonment, confusion, and doubt. We read as well of sorrow, regret, shame, and of course, grief.

The psalms contain the whole gamut of human emotion, and they give us words to voice our feelings to God.

A dear pastor in our area whose heart was shattered when his daughter and her friend committed suicide together shared with me how the prayers of lament that are contained in the psalms were helping him. Our conversation stirred my curiosity, and I began reading the psalms through new eyes, looking specifically for the psalms of lament.

To *lament* is "to mourn aloud, to express sorrow, to cry out in grief."[8] Some estimate that one out of every three psalms are songs of lament. So a third of the Jewish hymnbook was comprised of songs in the minor key as Israel wrestled with their pain. Add to that the book of Lamentations, large parts of the book of Jeremiah, and almost all of Job, and it becomes apparent that God is trying to tell us something—or rather, trying to help us tell Him something. He does not reject our prayers of grief, and He even provides us with examples of godly people who came to Him in their grief and gives us the words they prayed.

Some may wonder why there is so much lament in the Bible, but the reason is pretty simple. There is so much lament in the Bible because there is so much pain in our lives.

When we express our lament, we release our grief through raw, heartfelt, authentic prayer to our God who loves us, cares about us, and is willing to hear us out without chastising us. Some may be hesitant to pray with the same kind of honesty and openness as the psalmists did for fear of feeling irreverent or disrespectful. But the very fact that they kept praying was an expression of faith. As one author stated, "Giving God the silent treatment is the ultimate manifestation of unbelief. Despair lives under the hopeless resignation that God doesn't care, he doesn't hear, and nothing is ever going to change. People who believe this stop praying. They give up."[9]

Some may be hesitant to release their grief through prayerful lament for fear of their prayers being perceived as complaining. After reading of the times Israel complained and was chastised for it, we want no part of that. The prayers of lament in Scripture, however, show us the difference between complaining in unbelief (as the Israelites did in the wilderness) and bringing our complaints to God in honesty and faith. When we pray through the prayers of the lament in the Bible, we see that they contain both the expression of grief and statements of truth about God. They become a model for wrestling through the tension between our experience and God's goodness. That these godly people in Scripture would pray at all was an expression of faith. And how they did it is a pattern for us.

I encourage you to use the words of the psalms to express your grief and trust to the Lord.

Receive help from others. One of the most common human reactions to pain is to isolate ourselves from others. But, as we saw in the previous chapter, God intends that other people be one of the means by which He comforts our hearts.

Even the great apostle Paul was comforted by human presence. A few chapters before telling the Corinthian church about his thorn in the flesh, he described a time when "our flesh had no rest, but we were troubled on every side; without were fightings, within were fears" (2 Corinthians 7:5). Yes, even Paul had times of struggle and vulnerability. And how did God help him? He shares in the next verse: "Nevertheless God, that comforteth those that are cast down, comforted us by the coming of Titus."

Remember how discouraged Elijah was after facing down the prophets of Baal on Mt. Carmel? When he heard that Jezebel was trying to kill him he ran into the desert alone. There he complained bitterly to God that he was alone. When we're hurting, we are not always at our most rational. The reason Elijah was alone is that he refused help. "And when he saw that, he arose, and went for his life, and came to Beersheba, which belongeth to Judah, *and left his servant there*" (1 Kings 19:3). There are times when we need to be alone to pour out our hearts to the Lord. Solitude can be healthy. But there is a difference between solitude (simply being alone) and isolation (cutting others out of our lives). We must not isolate ourselves from others.

Even Jesus in His greatest hour of grief did not cut Himself off from others. The Bible records that as Jesus went to the Garden of Gethsemane to pray, He brought three of His closest disciples and plainly shared the sorrow of His soul.

And he took with him Peter and the two sons of Zebedee, and began to be sorrowful and very heavy. Then saith he unto them, My soul is exceeding sorrowful, even unto death: tarry ye here, and watch with me. And he went a little further, and fell on his face, and prayed, saying, O my Father, if it be possible, let this cup pass from me: nevertheless not as I will, but as thou wilt. (Matthew 26:37–39)

Jesus experienced the brunt of sorrow and heaviness—an unspeakable heaviness that even His disciples could not understand. In fact, they ultimately slept instead of praying with Him. Yet Jesus wanted the nearness of their presence and honestly expressed the need of His soul.

Surrender to God's will. The words of Jesus' prayer in the Garden of Gethsemane provide another tool for us in responding to grief: surrender. Three times Jesus prayed, "nevertheless not as I will, but as thou wilt."

Surrender is, in a sense, another word for acceptance. But it's a fuller kind of acceptance—the acceptance that not only receives the reality of loss, but that also chooses to trust God's decisions.

Jesus' example shows us that surrender isn't a one-and-done decision. It is a decision we make over and over. Matthew 26:44 says, "And he left them, and went away again, and prayed the third time, *saying the same words.*" Don't be discouraged when you find yourself coming back to the place of surrender over and over. But don't resist it either. Instead, follow Jesus' example and be willing to repeatedly pray, "O my Father, if it be possible, let this cup pass from me: nevertheless not as I will, but as thou wilt. ... O my Father, if this cup may not pass away from me, except I drink it, thy will be done" (Matthew 26:39, 42).

Enough Is Not the Same as Easy

There is no easy path through grief. Yes, God's grace is sufficient—it is enough. It helps and upholds us. It ministers to the deepest places of our souls.

But that doesn't mean our path is easy. Grief is still hard. It hurts. Sometimes the emotional pain is so severe that you feel it physically.

I don't share this to discourage you, but to encourage you on the path of receiving God's grace. Don't be alarmed when the way is not easy. Instead, pour out your heart to God, receive the help He sends, and surrender your will to His. In other words, receive God's sufficient grace for a hard path. It is enough, and it is good.

CONCLUSION

Why?

SOME PEOPLE HAVE BEEN LED to believe that it is wrong to ask God "why?" when we are suffering. This assertion, however, doesn't square with Scripture. David questioned God numerous times in the psalms when seeking for answers. He questioned God many times, including these:

- When God seemed to be distant: "My God, my God, why hast thou forsaken me? why art thou so far from helping me, and from the words of my roaring?" (Psalm 22:1).

- When he felt forsaken by Him: "For thou art the God of my strength: why dost thou cast me off? why go I mourning because of the oppression of the enemy?" (Psalm 43:2).

- When he felt God had forgotten about him: "How long wilt thou forget me, O LORD? for ever? how long wilt thou hide thy face from me?" (Psalm 13:1).

- When he felt God was asleep: "Awake, why sleepest thou, O Lord? arise, cast us not off for ever" (Psam 44:23).

- When he felt God was hiding from him: "Hide not thy face far from me; put not thy servant away in anger: thou hast been my help; leave me not, neither forsake me, O God of my salvation" (Psalm 27:9).

- When he felt like injustice was going to be permitted to go on unpunished: "LORD, how long shall the wicked, how long shall the wicked triumph? How long shall they utter and speak hard things? and all the workers of iniquity boast themselves?" (Psalm 94:3–4).

God is not put off by our questions. Rather, our "why" questions allow us to go before our heavenly Father and pour out our hearts to Him. As one author observed, "'Why?' is the first and greatest question of the suffering soul."[10]

When we sprain an ankle, our body's natural reflex is to rush fluids to the area, causing swelling. It prepares the injured site for healing. But our bodies, in response to the trauma, can easily overdo the reaction. This is why medical professionals instruct us to control the swelling with ice and pressure. In much the same way, questions are the soul's natural response to pain, and God knows that. He knows they are part of the process of healing.[11]

Even so, there is a danger in a persistent focus on why. There is a difference in asking "why?" as the overflow of our anguish and asking "why?" as a demand that God provide us with a satisfactory reason for our pain. Look again at the verses above as David questioned God. His questions were intense, and he hoped for answers. But they were not ultimatums that if God didn't answer, David would turn away from the Lord.

If we focus on the question of "why?" and anticipate that God will give us a satisfactory reason for the pain, we will be disappointed. Furthermore, the longer our demand goes unanswered, the more it feeds a sense of entitlement. As that sense of entitlement grows, it usually leads to bitterness.

The reality is that at the end of the day, an explanation from God is not going to satisfy me. It wouldn't change anything. It would just lead to more questions. So my constant prayer is this: "God, help my faith and trust in You to be greater than my need to know why."

And I have been learning that, while the question of *why* is permissible, it doesn't usually lead to comfort or bring a sense of conclusion. Instead, I've been asking God questions of *how*. How might God use this trial to glorify Himself? How might God use these hard circumstances to show me something about Him? How might God use my pain for His purpose? How might God use this chaos to make me into a man who walks by faith not by sight? To show me that true peace is found only in Him?

I love this poem by A. M. Overton that reminds me that God doesn't make mistakes.

My Father's way may twist and turn,
My heart may throb and ache,
But in my soul I'm glad I know,
He maketh no mistake.

My cherished plans may go astray,
My hopes may fade away,
But still I'll trust my Lord to lead
For He doth know the way.

Though night be dark and it may seem
That day will never break;
I'll pin my faith, my all in Him,
He maketh no mistake.

There's so much now I cannot see,
My eyesight's far too dim;
But come what may, I'll simply trust
And leave it all to Him.

For by and by the mist will lift
And plain it all He'll make,
Through all the way, though dark to me,
He made not one mistake.

Did Paul ever receive an answer for why he was given a thorn in the flesh? In a way, yes. He received at least a partial answer that God was using that suffering to bring about humility and dependance on God's strength. But that wasn't a specific answer for his specific type of suffering. After all, Paul had other suffering in his life too. Could God not have used those things to accomplish His purposes? Yes, but He didn't. So Paul chose to accept God's choices.

Better still, Paul discovered God's grace. In fact, when Paul understood the sufficiency of God's grace, he made a connection between grace for the need he originally brought to God in prayer and grace for every other need of his life:

"And he said unto me, My grace is sufficient for thee: for my strength is made perfect in weakness. Most gladly therefore will I rather glory in my infirmities, that the power of Christ may rest upon me. Therefore I take pleasure in infirmities, in reproaches, in necessities, in persecutions, in distresses for Christ's sake: for when I am weak, then am I strong" (2 Corinthians 12:9–10).

Friend, I don't know what grief you may be experiencing, and I surely don't know why God has allowed it in your life. But I do know two truths:

1. You don't have to get over it.
2. God's grace can lead you through it.

Trust Him, and receive His all-sufficient grace.

Eternal Life

A FTER T. J.'S FUNERAL, a lady named Sally introduced herself to Katie and me. She was a young mom who knew T. J. and shared how grateful she was for the way his funeral service had honored the important things to him—his family and the Lord. But there was more. You see, at the funeral, T. J.'s pastor had told the congregation that T. J. was in Heaven— not because he was a good man, but because he had chosen to receive God's gift of eternal life. Sally shared with us that she had not previously had assurance that if she were to die in a sudden accident, like T. J., that she would be in Heaven. But that day, while seated in T. J.'s funeral, Sally understood what the Bible says about eternal life and put her trust in Christ as her personal Savior. Katie and I were thrilled for her and thankful for how the Lord was continuing to use T. J.'s life to point others to Him.

Perhaps you are in Sally's position. You have lost someone or something you love and at the same time have questions about your own eternal destiny. Where will you go when your life on Earth ends?

As we conclude these pages, I would love to share with you what T. J.'s pastor shared at his funeral so you too may have assurance of eternal life and a personal relationship with Jesus Christ.

Some people think we can't really know for sure where we will go when we die. But in the Bible, God tells us that He wants us to *know* we have eternal life.

> These things have I written unto you that believe on the name of the Son of God; that ye may know that ye have eternal life, and that ye may believe on the name of the Son of God. (1 John 5:13)

If God wants us to know we have eternal life, why is it that not everyone does? Why is it that everyone doesn't just automatically go to Heaven? The answer is simple: we are all sinners.

God is a perfect, holy God. And no matter how hard we try to measure up, we still fall short of God's standard of perfection. The Bible says we all fall short of the glory of God.

> As it is written, There is none righteous, no, not one... For all have sinned, and come short of the glory of God; (Romans 3:10, 23)

Furthermore, sin comes with a payment—eternal death, separation from God in Hell. Romans 6:23 says, "For the wages of sin is death..." You see, the wages, or payment, of sin is not good works, as many people assume. We don't "make up" for our sin or "balance the scales" by our goodness. Ephesians 2 makes this clear:

> For by grace are ye saved through faith; and that not of yourselves: it is the gift of God: Not of works, lest any man should boast. (Ephesians 2:8–9)

Instead, God offers us forgiveness and eternal life as a *gift.*

> For the wages of sin is death, but the gift of God is eternal life through Jesus Christ our Lord. (Romans 6:23)

Eternal life is a free gift that is only available through Jesus Christ. You see, when Jesus died on the cross, He was not paying for His own sin—He was God and did not sin. He was paying for *our* sin.

> But God commendeth his love toward us, in that, while we were yet sinners, Christ died for us. (Romans 5:8)

Remember, the payment for sin is death—and that's exactly what Jesus paid. He died for our sin, rose from the grave three days later, and now offers us forgiveness of sin and eternal life as a gift. You don't earn it or achieve it. You simply put your faith in Jesus Christ and in His payment for your sin.

In order to have a relationship with Christ and an eternal home in Heaven, we must stop trusting ourselves, our works, and our religions, and place our full trust in Jesus Christ alone for the forgiveness of our sin and eternal life.

> That if thou shalt confess with thy mouth the Lord Jesus, and shalt believe in thine heart that God hath raised him from the dead, thou shalt be saved. For with the heart man believeth unto righteousness; and with the mouth confession is made unto salvation.... For whosoever shall call upon the name of the Lord shall be saved. (Romans 10:9–10, 13)

That is a promise directly from God that if you will pray to Him, confess that you are a sinner, ask Him to forgive your sins, and turn to Him alone to be your Savior; He promises to save you and give you the free gift of eternal life. You can make that decision today by praying from your heart something like this:

> Dear God, I know that I am separated from you because of sin. I confess that in my sin, I cannot save myself. Right now, I turn to you alone to be my Savior. I ask you to save me from the penalty

of my sin, and I trust you to provide eternal life to me.—Amen

You might phrase that prayer in your own words. God just wants to hear you express an understanding of your need for Him, your trust in Him alone as your Savior from the penalty of sin, and your desire to have a relationship with Him and eternal life in Heaven.

If you have not yet trusted Christ as your Savior, I encourage you to do it *today* and change your life for all eternity. You will never regret it.

ENDNOTES

1   Jerry Sittser, *A Grace Disguised* (Grand Rapids: Zondervan, 1998), 62–63.

2   Dean Herring, "Little Feet," *The Blog of Pastor Dean Herring,* May 21, 2019, https://svbaptistchurch.wordpress.com/2019/05/21/little-feet/.

3   Quoted in *Giants of the Missionary Trail* (Chicago, IL: Scripture Press Foundation, 1954), 73.

4   Vance Havner, *Day by Day* (Westwood, NJ: Fleming H. Revell Company, 1953), entry for March 6.

5   Max Lucado, *Grace* (Nashville, TN: Thomas Nelson, 2012), 99.

6   Mary Winslow, *Christian Experience* (London: William Hunt and Company, 1868), 1.

7   John Kitchen, *Life as Worship* (Fort Washington, PA: CLC Publications, 2015), Kindle Edition.

8   *Merriam-Webster's Collegiate Dictionary,* Eleventh Edition (Springfield, MA: Merriam-Webster, Incorporated, 2004), 698.

9   Mark Vroegop, *Dark Clouds, Deep Mercy* (Wheaton, IL: Crossway, 2019), 32.

10 John Kitchen, *Life as Worship* (Fort Washington, PA: CLC Publications, 2015), Kindle Edition.

11 Ibid.

 BILL PRATER was reached for Christ as a teenager through the outreach of Fellowship Baptist Church in Liberal, Kansas. Five years later, he and his wife Katie were married and joined the full-time ministry staff of the same church. In 2000, the church called Bill to be the senior pastor—a position he filled for two decades. He now serves in an itinerant preaching ministry as a staff evangelist from Fellowship Baptist Church.

In addition to his ministry to Fellowship Baptist Church, Bill serves the community of Liberal as a board member and facilitator for the Leadership Enrichment and Development group, and as a chaplain for the Liberal Police Department.

Bill and his wife Katie have three adult children: T. J. (now in Heaven), Tyler, and Tiffany. In an answer to Bill and Katie's prayers, their daughter-in-law Sheena married another godly man, Derek. The Praters have eight grandchildren: Boston, Malorie, Kevin, Ellie, Huck, Callie, Leroy, and Turner.

ADDITIONAL BOOKS YOU MAY ENJOY...

The Burden Bearer by Paul Chappell

The allegory in these pages will captivate your heart and profoundly change your life. Follow the main character—Carrier—on his journey with the Burden Bearer, and discover the Christian life and relationship with Jesus that you were meant to enjoy!

A Maze of Grace by Paul Chappell

Claiming God's Grace during a Season of Suffering

If you are, or someone you love is, enduring a season of suffering, this little booklet will provide a cup of fresh water for the journey. Each chapter will share God's wisdom, encouragement, and insight. Each turn of the page will bring fresh hope and trust in the unseen hand of a loving God.

Bitter or Better by Don Sisk

Emerging Victorious Through Trials

If you knew that God could take the darkest circumstances of your life and turn them into the brightest joys, how would that affect your response to trials? Dr. Don Sisk examines why God allows heartaches in our lives and how our response determines our future usefulness. He explores four truths that can make the difference in trials.

STRIVINGTOGETHER.COM

ALSO AVAILABLE AS EBOOKS

ADDITIONAL BOOKS YOU MAY ENJOY...